Look at

by Shirley Horton

PEARSON

Scott
Foresman

Editorial Offices: Glenview, Illinois • Parsippany, New Jersey • New York, New York
Sales Offices: Needham, Massachusetts • Duluth, Georgia • Glenview, Illinois
Coppell, Texas • Sacramento, California • Mesa, Arizona

ISBN: 0-328-13145-8

5 6 7 8 9 10 V010 14 13 12 11 10 09 08 07

Look at Bix.

Look at Bix up in the van.

Look at Bix and the vet.

Look at Bix take the paper.

Look at Bix.

Some vets make medicine for pets. Dogs will take medicine that tastes like cheese. Cats will take medicine that tastes like fish. Birds will take medicine that tastes like fruit. What do you think medicine for rabbits tastes like?